Service Changes

Timothy Carroll

ISBN:0692721983
ISBN-13:9780692721988

Cover Art by: A. Ripley Design

This book is dedicated to those once deemed Lazy

CONTENTS

Cover Letter   i

From: New York City

Limbs   1

What Am I Doing   2

I am not a poet today.   3

Untitled   4

Higitus Figitus   5

February 27, 2010   6

Sleepy Hollow   7

Rifle   8

Poetry   9

On Returning from an Upstate Interview   11

Hunting   12

My Train Home is a Blind Bleeding Horse   13

Dream Deferred   14

21st Century Avenues   15

From My Window   16

For Lack of Sleeping   17

To: Minneapolis

It's Morning Again in America — 19

These Days — 21

I — 22

What a Mess — 23

Feelings — 25

Love Revisited — 26

Meatball Recipe — 28

Shine — 29

Sequels — 30

My 8Ball Thinks I'm Bitter — 31

A Deadman's 2013 — 32

I Hate Kenny G & the Dept. of Human Services — 34

Remember to Chew Your Food — 35

Christmas in Ferguson — 36

Telescope — 37

Things Wild — 38

To Those Who Bunt in Kickball — 39

Resume — 41

Timothy Carroll
2845 29th Ave. S
Minneapolis, MN 55406
(860) 921-1348
Tmc444@hotmail.com

February 29, 2016

New York Stock Exchange
20 Broad Street
New York, NY 10005

To Whom It May Concern:

As a thinker, I'm always trying to decide if life is miserable or wonderful: I have a son, a wife, we frolic about happily, I have friends that are inspiring and hilarious, and I have a good view of the stars from my backyard, so I decide easily, wonderful, absolutely. But in the morning, I go to work. If there is an anti-matter to Adult Life, and we all know there is— some dark unknown pulling our reveries apart— it has to be what we know today as the 8 hour work day. For kids, it's that box we stuff them into called school—

But I like my job, actually, which I am starting to think is the problem. Why should I like my job? My friends can't come. My most superior superior doesn't even have a view of the stars so what is there to aspire to? A Fact: No Monday morning meeting will ever mention the recent discoveries in our solar system, which, to me, is an unacceptable reality. And thus, a miserable one.

As a lucky person with an enjoyable job, it's easy to get distracted for 50 years and completely forget the contents of the galaxy. Once in a while, when I find myself blissfully lost in the woods, I remember my life and the scale of the universe and fall to my knees and die. Because that is what is happening now, Death, right after I get out of work, that is. Work is now, Death is now, and life is the 2 week vacation somewhere cheap and sunny, which I recall nothing about except that it was in Florida.

Respectfully,

Timothy Carroll

From: New York City

Limbs

There is a tool used in clothing stores that assists workers in folding shirts. It is a board much like the cutting board I use to prepare my dinners on. I suppose I could use the cutting board to fold clothes, but would run the risk of eating my collared shirts or staining the whites with tomatoes. Somehow, thanks to my time at Eddie Bauer, I can now maintain order in my dresser as well as cleanly chop off the limbs of a well-dressed chicken.

What Am I Doing

I spend my days
My beautiful days

Lining filthy floors
Of department stores
With industrial red tape

My boss
Is a motherfucker at minimum
Wage

I assist
Dumbfounded customers
With utmost urgency

Because I too
Feel the value
Of time

And I too
Do not want to be here
Any longer

So just please
Help me

Get what I need
So I can hit
The road
My man

I am not a poet today.

Today I am an observer, listener, jammer/toe-tapper
   to my music, a street walker, avoider of slimy hepatitis rails.
I was a poet, a few weeks ago, I remember.
I was The Poet of my lifetime, on a bench, in a campground,
   under the most ruthless hornets' nest ever heard.
That day I was all fire, preparing a message for the people; writing carbon
   letters that will be— or should be— fossilized for the future moon exodus
   or at least my curious grandchildren.
But that was some time ago.
Today I am the guy who will give up his seat to the elderly, the guy who
   should buff the gaze from his eyes and be ware of oncoming traffic.
Today I am waiting for dinner, waiting for a phone call from my friend Ethan,
   waiting for my other selves to pay me a surprise visit,
    to be led through the gates
                    by that poet.

Untitled

At night you come to me when I'm quiet. You're excited
and brilliant but I roll over because I need my nine
hours. I'll get back to you tomorrow, I promise.
But by then you will have left early. By then

you will have changed— losing your
inventive out of space zigzag lust
for purity because the morning
is made of numbing habits.

Why don't I listen
to you. You say,
why don't you
lie down and
listen to
me?

Higitus Figitus

In a time of grace-filled goodness
    and thick
        dark
          evil
             there is a need for magic.
The difference between white
              and black magic in such a time
is that the white for example
    could give one wings
        poof one into a sparrow,
           and that's fun.
      One can venture off to exciting places with wings,
             a belly full of joy-worms.
Whereas black magic (not
    to be confused with the black hawk, which is real
                 and
    wired to dart for the neck) can zap life from a flower.
Can it zap the life back in? Probably
    (just as it can change from warthog to princess)
            but don't count on it.
In a world of wizards' duels, wherein
        pink
         elephants
          run
from blue mice,
      one side must be rammed over the edge by the other
because the townsfolk have a dire need to bow.
      Who can pull this sword from this stone?

February 27, 2010

The second to last strange day of February

    has the city's train-tracks buzzing cold.

I would stay inside with my thin winter legs

    but the forecast tells I won't be here forever.

 That I should get out. Be always out. Canoeing

    through denizen courtyards, apartment-office buildings.

Jiving with musicians about the sunflower in their soul.

Asking benched strangers open-ended questions. Where are you going?

Where have you been out west, and why? What things

    do you feel most confident about?

I am very much a brain-cloud in the city's gray-day

    trying to absorb the precious street metals before I move upstate

    to the quietland, and grow old for real this time.

Sleepy Hollow

Sleepy Hollow High sits proudly
atop a hill gazing at the Hudson River.
A sign reads: Thanks for the Funding!
in a tone I hear coming from a poolside choir
of ungrateful adolescent brats.
What could I, a rogue pedagogue
from Broke City, have taught them?

Today I am headless!
charging maniacally late past this scene
panicking to find Rockefeller
in Rockefeller's "Playhouse"
where I am to serve him and associates
exquisite hors d'oeuvres.

I will do this, of course,

but with the bubbling red rage
and fiery tongue of a marauder misunderstood,
wailing for justice, howling for my head
to be returned as it once was
secured, rosy, forward-looking

while also praying that Dick and these gentlemen
tip handsomely
with crisp letters of recommendation—
the generals' orders—
and off I go
galloping back to that school
wielding a razor sharp
resume.

Rifle

My grandfather sold his rifle soon after he got back.
   I thought, damn wouldn't that be something to have;
          to hold, smell—
                   the deranged cold
                   of an Austrian winter
                   whirling in the haunted void of the barrel.
Wouldn't that be something
to pass on to my children.

Poetry
for Lou Asekoff

I read once that Baseball is not Poetry
    no matter how badly men want it to be. But the names: Shoeless Jo
    Jackson, Satchel Paige, Cool Papa Bell sure is.

Poetry is not so much an airplane as it is the take-off
    with everyone getting outta town, shot straight towards the sun.

Poetry is not money
    unless in coin form and tip-toed down a dark alley in black bags.

Poetry is not a police car,
    but it is a firetruck.

Walt Whitman did not become Poetry
    until the first beard hair sprung grey,
    and Thoreau, the moment his cell door slammed shut.

Poetry is not Hillary Clinton
    until she admits to being a werewolf, so we'll see.

Poetry is rain & thunder,
    and lightning bolts pound Poetry back into the Earth.

Somehow sexy women in sexy short dresses aren't Poetry anymore—

Poetry is the grandparent,
    their wrinkles the most sincere couplets.

Poetry is midnight,
    not 9 or 5 o'clock. It is not brushing your teeth or starting your car.

Poetry is not this poem
    unless you agree 1,000% with at least one thing.

Poetry is not birds
    as it is the dream of flying (our flyingblues, freedomblues).

Poetry is ALL sounds EXCEPT Kenny G,
    and that includes busy signals and air-raids.

Poetry is trees,
    of all heights, at all times— swaying, frozen, falling— you can't
    beat'em.

Strangely enough, Poetry is bad news
    which is the good news.

Poetry is the art of not understanding,
    but you want to.

Motorcycles, black-smoke-puffing trains,
    old Mississippi's paddle boats, all run on high octane poetry.
    But cars, rockets, battleships, Sherman tanks, do not— Taxis do.

Forgotten Poetry lives in abandoned train stations.

Poetry is the past but not the future,
    and the right-nows are dangerously on the fence.

Poetry is the sudden end leaving you dying
    either of loneliness or acceptance.

On Returning from an Upstate Interview

A hellfire route through reality:
From arrogant handshakes of suburban principals, to speeding train
with well-dressed commuters, through enchanted Westchester forest, to
sudden shock of Bronx as if slapped from a fairytale, to Langston's
Harlem, pride of poverty, home to King NYCHA the Merciful, sitting on
his throne of vouchers, to bus that drags its worried load along 125th
obstacles, to Robert Kennedy's steal rainbow

--The Bridge--
Bus running for its life, screams past the loonies on Randall's Island.

That horrible prison with perfect skyline view for its lonely captives is the
city's final warning: Keep Cool. You don't want to do anything crazy in
this town. I shudder at the thought of its endless halls and cling to
Ginsberg. "Paterson" has me in tears for us all and all the nervous hours
and years past. Off in Queens, my worn black shoes walk my way home.
I wonder, who is walking with me? Walking walking walking like marching
feet.

Hunting

Another noon-day job hunt
when the sun is a devil
and the steaming pavement melts my soles.

Each city block is guarded
by young gangsters
water-gunning people down in the street,
threatening to put me **out!**

There is nowhere to hide
from an urban July
when broke.

They know this
but don't know they know it.

So we sweat it out.

My Train Home is a Blind Bleeding Horse

Its tunnel is a torture chamber
      of radioactive lights and electric eels
Its speed
    a handicapped typhoon that drank way too much

Its conductor
    the Big Bad Wolf trying to earn a buck
Its passengers
    blood clots with coagulating temperaments
              their faces
         cold noodle soup
Its fare
    one bladder infection

My train home jerks back and forth like a crocodile's tail

Its screams
    the bludgeoning of a quiet evening

Its announcement
     eventually

It has teenagers like measles

Its windows
    my dreams splashed with mud
Its seats
    expired Flintstone vitamins

Its advertisements are sons of bitches

My train home
    has wheels of false tarnished teeth

Its smell is a pink slip

Its lighting December's 6:30am

Its destination
    Unknown

Dream Deferred

My pup chirps in her sleep.
Her paws do spastic sprints.
I know she dreams of Kentucky
and the farm from whence she came—
running towards her mama
in the gentle June grass.

I'll wake her with a creek of morning floor
and see the deep disappointment in her eye.

She'll lay in bed all day and huff and puff
before starting the second shift
guarding my home
monitoring the city street.

21st Century Avenues

Saved by the few quasi-living
intellectual halfzies met through poetry
with hand-me-down eyes
occupying thick-skinned ghettos—

Where are all the Emma Goldmans
Thoreaus
Rosa Luxemburgs
Whitmans
Ginsbergs
eating at the spine of a generation?

Where do they hide or where are they buried?
In the gutters of stomachs, I suppose.
I hear little

but the refrain of workers workers workers workers workers workers
workers workers workers workers workers workers workers workers
workers workers workers workers workers workers workers workers
workers workers workers workers workers workers workers workers
workers workers workers workers workers workers workers workers
workers workers workers workers workers workers workers workers
workers workers workers workers workers workers workers workers
workers workers workers workers workers workers workers workers
workers workers workers workers workers workers workers workers
workers workers workers workers workers workers workers workers
workers workers workers workers workers workers workers workers
workers workers workers workers workers workers workers workers
workers workers workers workers workers workers workers workers
workers workers workers workers workers workers workers workers
workers workers workers workers workers workers workers workers
workers workers workers workers workers workers workers workers
workers workers workers workers workers workers workers workers
workers workers workers workers workers workers workers workers
workers workers workers workers workers workers workers workers
workers workers workers workers workers workers workers workers
workers workers workers workers workers workers workers workers
workers workers workers workers workers workers workers workers
workers workers workers workers workers workers workers workers
workers workers workers workers workers workers workers workers
workers workers workers workers workers workers workers workers
workers workers workers workers workers workers workers workers

From My Window

while I sit and ponder language
for a cover letter
wishing I was a wildfire
or something else

a motor-bike fires past 1,000 MPH,
a silver bullet shot from the urban gut
into the dark unknown.

No temperature in summer's night.
Just a nude indifferent breeze, expelled
from some stormy, sub-tropic paradise.

For Lack of Sleeping

movable unman comes tacit courting
        groans a mediaeval Uh

pale ember invades the eyes

between this frill rhythm and the hemisphere
the thievish week blows the skull open HUFF

which he falls into like a tenfold hole
        mixing iodine to a loony's wit

as the brain-legs stumble for everyday train
        mouth parts with a tonic-dove Eh
            which is swiftly picked by a sly panhandler
                            muffled by
                      WOOF

A façade-sphere points on Ramble Avenue

walking under suncloud or dragged through ranting red fog
        the phantom's face wilts
            feels the atomic weight of his clothes

the mind a lofty thought-pit honks
        at passing philanderers
            their nifty tendons
                basement apes with sweetening growls

the deaf sun shushing all this puttering

he reaches the descending stairs
        flops down
            a fishy decrescendo

                      sits the sorrows
                      the ill-fated wait

To: Minneapolis

It's Morning Again in America

A chicken in every pot   a car in every garage
Are you better off than a rejuvenated horse

Leave no child in the garage
Leave no chicken in the pail
Vote yourself cool
He's making us cool again
He's making us chickens again
America needs garages not just peanuts

America needs horses in their garageses
Change we can feed to a horse
Change we can put in a pail
Yes   Peanuts

Building a bridge to future horses
The stakes are too American
Farms are soo four years ago
Let America eat peanuts from a pail
There's normalcy in cocktails
Don't swap a child in the middle of a stream
Keep cool in the garage
Yes   We Cool
Yes   We Vote
Let America be cool again

Are you better off than Nixon
Don't stop thinking about Country
Building a bridge to Nixon's garage
Horses for a better America
Farms need garages   pails   and chickens
Don't stop putting people in pails
Who is James K Polk?

It's morning again in America
A chicken in every car   a stake in every child
Are you better off with no child
Don't stop thinking about chicken farm
America needs real plans for real horses
A chicken in every child
Putting people first   **Country First**   people in garages
With real change and chickens
Chickens thinking about tomorrow
Chickens keep cool with horses

19

Horses for change
Americans need a pail of horse stake
He is making us proud again

Who is James K Polk?
A future 21st century cock farmer
Building a bridge out of American families
Yes   we can change Americanz into automatic garages
Yes we can
The stakes are too cool not to

Future horses eat left behind children
Making us proud again
Are you better off than a farm pail
Yes   America needs cool futures
Yes   cox and cocktails are better for the nation

He's making us dinner again
Hope stakes we can believe in
Real plans for cool people

Don't swap yourself for American Nixons
A bridge to the future ends with a garage of chickens

These Days

Stirring tornadoes cause sirens to warn Minnesotans
just like the Cold War did for my parents before me,
and like bombers did for grandpa in his bunker, asleep.

There's never a tornado or even a breeze
causing me to duck, genetically.

The siren shouldn't be used
when Russians are on the move
and while my sky is benignly blue.

Though, one never knows with tornadoes
what they may harvest and send forth
from our old Midwest silos.

I

I am

I am a teacher

I am a teacher but

I am a teacher but I can't

I am a teacher but I can't find a teaching job

I am a teacher but I can't find a teaching job so

I sell baking goods that are mass produced in Hong Kong

I sell baking goods that are mass produced

I sell baking goods

Baking goods

Sell baking goods

Baking goods

Sell

What a Mess

I'm not full of myself
but I spend more time thinking about my hair
than I do thinking about Iraq.

I think about Iraq a lot, actually,
especially in my car
or walking my dog,

but I glance at my hair every chance I get.
Whether to cut it down or grow it
takes much consideration and much time, which I give it.

But the fact is, I don't give a shit.
My hair is a lose-lose situation.
It's thinning out and that's just fine.

But then again, if I leave it to its own devices
it becomes a hot mess,
then I'm not happy, my wife's not happy,

and she tries to style it by force
in unnatural ways that looks dumb,
makes me feel dumb,

and I think everyone is looking
at me like, "dude, what are you doing?
You touching it makes it infinitely worse!"

The idea of someone thinking that fills my day
with worry and indecision...
I don't know.

But, I should think, who cares what anyone thinks?
I'm not paying $30 for a legit haircut,
I'll do it myself.

And besides, are you kidding me?
Who cares?
Iraq is murdering itself!

And I let this happen;
I paid for this,
because I don't give much consideration

to what happens after my wars.
Iraq should be on my mind.
Iraq should be on my mind.

But my hair,
goddamn it, is a travesty
and dying for a solution.

Feelings
for Amy Ripley

1

Amy, We feel you could be more

                      Dedicated, Focused, Goal-oriented,
                      Driven, Cooperative, Innovative,
                      Organized, Efficient, Engaged,
                      Can-do, Dependable, Effective,
                      Flexible, Enthusiastic, Assertive

2

Tim, I'm just so

                      Pissed-off, Drained, Speechless,
                      Offended, Overlooked, Overwhelmed,
                      Disrespected, Disgusted, Ignored,
                      Beyond-hope, Taken-advantage-of,
                      Hurt, Shocked, Tired-of-their-bullshit,
                      & Worn-out

Love Revisited

I met you as a young man on London
cobblestone. You were such my type
of mystery I let you make a wanderer
out of me. We mingled with cathedrals
and danced with the ghosts of knights.
I was struck by the exotic arrow and
bled out America.

What can a dazzle-dumbd lover do
with a foreign nymph but tumble
over her in the eternal grass?
Sprinting to open every door,
losing ourselves in the adventure maze,
never to return.

In a violent flash I found myself
hurling back towards Boston,
leaving you in the arms of some
other giddy virgin Yank.

A year later, I leapt at the chance
to meet you under the thick legs
of the Eiffel Tower. Looking exactly
the same, you seized me
with your long warm tongue
and the tower glimmered gold
salvation! We strolled like the
Seine, fornicating with everything
Parisian. We came to an
understanding: never to leave
each other again.

Kicking and screaming back towards JFK,
I wept into a salesman's lap.
You refused to elope to my squirrely
New England woods.
I didn't understand and went home to live
in a foggy depression

for several debilitating years,
shedding years at familial stoplights,
shopping malls.

Finally we met again outside an eastern
port. Our eyes met as those Asian doors
opened sucking me out into the humid-spiced
air of the sub-continent.
You raced me to a wailing run-away bus.
I hopped on and was immediately robbed.
You paid our thief for his services
with all your jewelry from African travels.
We held onto each other, entwining
every limb, and disappeared into the Jungle.

We rented a flat six hours from any airplane
so as not to get separated ever again.
We spent years teaching orphans,
riding slow trains, drinking tea with farmers.
We raised a baby elephant who would carry
us from village to Brahmaputra for fishing
and swim. We were branded married
by the elders. We never felt alone again.

*

If you are reading this, my truest love,
I am sorry and alone. Like a fool, I strayed
during the storm, and awoke on the banks
of the Mississippi. I got a job selling cupcakes
for a mid-sized company in Minnesota.
Everyone is very nice, though the language
is confusing and frustrating.
I can't stand being apart. But, my dear angelic muse,
my renegade heart, you must go on without me.
I'm afraid I'm already too poor and fragile
to meet you atop the steps of Machhapuchre.

Meatball Recipe

I need 2 large eggs to start my day

1 c. dank coffee to grease the limbs

A pinch of afternoon forecast

½ oz. tooth whitening toothpaste

2 tbsp. spit

1 long reflection——

A drop of sticky hair stuff

4 qt. American dressing

2 c. worn out shoe

A speck of goodbye kiss

6 pt. of key jangling

3 tbsp. Morning Radio

10 lbs. of traffic

1 large yawn

A sprinkle of construction lights (yellow)

1 c. red light daydream...

5 tsp. **Honk!**

3 pts. No Parking Tuesdays & Thursdays

1 deep breath in beautiful silence

A dash of moldy "Good Morning"

Preheat to 350 degrees F under July sun; Cook in brick oven for 8 hrs; In a large mixing bowl, mix together into one large meatball; Mixture will yield approx. 9-5 servings; Serve warm

Shine

Being newly unemployed, I was selected to attend a job search training at my local Work Force Center or risk having my unemployment benefits canceled. An old bald man, I daydream is the guy from The Shining, is teaching us some valuable things:

Job searching today is all about networking, 75% of it, anyway, he says.
Strike 1, I shine. I'm relatively new to this town and the only people I know are poets and softball players.
Our eyes lock as he shines:

I bet you think you got an amazing resume...that all you got to do is spread it throughout the world and someone will snatch it up and give you an interview, ain't that right?
You're Goddamn right, that's exactly what I think.

Strike 2, he glares back. Ain't nobody impressed with what they read on paper no more. So you looked after that hotel for the winter, got some writing done, never desecrated a burial ground, fine! You think that makes you special?
Now I've hit an all-time low because I thought being telepathic, by definition, proves I AM special.

You strikin' out, Dock! Shinin' ain't just about doing good and mind reading. You gotta edit each resume to fit the job. You gotta go to job fairs and show these people you mean business! Take a part-timer if you gotta.
I tell him, I don't know, I'm only interested in writing, and maybe I'll apply to be the groundskeeper this summer. They must employ like twenty people to keep that maze looking proper.
He looks at me a long time. I love his shiny bald head.

Boy, you gonna be unemployed a long while with that attitude, a long, long while.
I ask him if I could just come in whenever I want to use the typewriter and make copies. His jaw drops, eyes widen, and slowly steps back as if I had just done something truly horrible.

Sequels

Life with America is a Godzilla marathon:
cycles of zen normalcy wrecked by fire-breathing monsters,
unthinkable screams.
The populace run left run right,
a president addresses the nation, the tanks roll.

After a decade, our wars today are winding down.

Godzilla, bored by murder mischief, goes to lie in country,
appearing in time to be, not a sleeping giant,
but a tranquil range of green hills.

And how time passes in mundane peace.

A generation grows in a land enchanted,
the elderly develop Alzheimer's,
and none suspect they have a serious Godzilla problem——————————

It is important to remember
a truly awesome villain is only temporarily unconscious.

And it is important to remember
there have been 60+ Godzilla movies.

And it is important to   remember
and remain conscious

of our hills in the distance,
swaying gently in the breeze,

or heaving.

My 8Ball Thinks I'm Bitter

Roll the Dice

To Hell With It

Nude Protest?

Play Dead

Wake Up!

Forgive.

Follow Their Lead

Swim

What Do You Want!?

Chomsky Gets It

Things Will Change

A Deadman's 2013

A relatively big year, I suppose. I had a steady, yet awful, job at Gardner Studios in Stillwater, MN, from April of last year to this past February, working as a Sales Coordinator, a deep ring in job-hell. The first day on the job I was handed what looked like a lifetime stack of fresh business cards with my name and title, and I instantly thought of grandpa and his lifetime of selling U.S. Steel, and how he is today broke and bludgeoned by medical bills.

On the bright side, my sales job was a window to 1) get out of credit card debt— which, at its height, reached $8,000— and 2) start saving for the down payment for a house. Cas and I saved $6,000 and bought a foreclosed house in South Minneapolis in February for $145,000. On our 5th year anniversary (Feb. 9th) Cassie and her dad left for a 2 week trip to Vietnam and then on to Cambodia to work at an elephant sanctuary. Towards the end of that month I was laid off from my Sales job and spent March and April painting our ceilings while collecting unemployment and job searching.

I had given up on trying to find a teaching job as my MN license was soon to expire unless I completed 2 additional years of Bachelor level Communications classes. I still can't get over the idea of having a MFA in Poetry and having the state tell me I need to get a minor in Communications to be qualified to teach English.

So I decided to focus on getting back into non-profit work. Grant writing and youth development jobs were ideal. For 2 months I applied for at least 4 jobs every day, as was my goal, and was rewarded with 2 interviews. Luckily— and I mean literal Luck— I got a job as a case manager for people suffering from mental illness for $34,000/yr. Crap pay, but having insurance for the first time in 5 years and the ability to pay a mortgage— 1/2 a mortgage, anyway— feels like I've been freed from a minimum security prison sentence. It really, really feels like that.

The strange thing, though, is that I haven't been able to shake off the accrued weight of anguish that has come with 3 dark years of no or malemployment and weekly job rejections. I used to be such a great shaker. Some bullshit comes along and there's nothing a steady dose of Bob Marley, Jack Kerouac, and a burger at Yankees stadium couldn't handle. But now, Kerouac's just a sad drunk, the Steinbrenners have ruined the game, and Bob, the happy guru from my youth, just another cancer victim.

I imagine a mild dose of PTSD feels somewhat like this. I feel that I have become, and am stuck being, an aged and bitterly tired version of myself. There is definitely a sense of hopelessness towards big aspirations and a growing demon of cynicism in me, yelling and complaining, constantly complaining about society and all its life-sucking institutions.

I hope it is like PTSD in that I could get past this over time and this isn't what is to become of my post-30 life. And I think I will become more positive throughout this summer with the help of warm weather, softball, and fixing up the house. Last week I booked a week of camping at Glacier National Park for this August, and what better place for a spiritual rebirth? Can't fucking wait.

I Hate Kenny G & the Dept. of Human Services
Note from Wikipedia: He was also an early investor in the Starbucks
coffee house chain.

Kenny G, while I sit on hold for the past 13 years
trying to prevent eviction and suicide,
you have not once answered and asked, "how may I help you?"

I know the sunsets on Key West

are warm and beautiful year round
and the women are mesmerizing
with their wavy blond hair in the breeze.
You remind me several times a day.

But wake up. It's not 1987,
you can't redeem food stamps for pina-coladas,
the bus doesn't run from Baltimore to Barbados and you're no Coltrane,
so put away your goddamn sunshine and pick up!

Or at least just play it like it is: rainy, cold, bus is late.

Remember to Chew Your Food

Did the dog shit this morning?
Jesus, did I?
Cassie yells at me because I keep forgetting
our baby's due date.
It's Aug. 16th.

Writing on yellow paper stimulates the memory
I remember reading in college.
Remember to call Em
and congratulate her on making the Honor Roll;
Call a guy about the furnace before the house blows up.
The baby IS due Aug. 16th.

I overheard a man on the radio
or in the gym talking about his sister.
She had Alzheimer's and forgot how to swallow and died!
I develop a quick self-diagnostic:

How old is grandpa? 93. Mom? 64. 64?
Dad had a seizure on my birthday in 2007,
mom called when I was out to dinner at that
Ethiopian place in Soho with that chick—she's at Yale now
studying International Law… was at Yale.
I went to a Firestone Tire protest with her outside the…
some famous hotel in Midtown.
The Plaza. The Waldorf Astoria, yup, first time I saw it.
Why were we protesting? Faulty tires killing mini-van families?
Manufacturing conditions in India—
I was protesting not getting laid all year, I know I know that—
she got arrested somehow, I went home alone.
She had a cat, Emma! (Boom! Remembering.)
Emma Goldman, which I thought was so sexy-revolutionary—
the cat wasn't sexy.

Always remember
the big difference between forgetting dates and how to shit.
(And the difference between there & their
and then & than.)

Remember to write this down:
your parents were good to you;
grandpa whistled when he walked and beat cancer thrice;
travel stops the aging process
while fear keeps you alive.

Christmas in Ferguson

Merry Christmas to the people of Ferguson
who prey on this very Christmas day for understanding—

Merry Christmas to the police and legislators of Saint Louis County
rising on this dawn of redeeming grace—

— A Miracle —

Awaken! To a fresh glistening
of snow & understanding across the kingdom:

though cold, with nowhere else to go
and buried up to our necks,

every one of us is trying to be good.
Nobody is asking for gifts of gold & silver

or light blue convertibles,
but good paying jobs,

good schools for the little ones,
and a big box of diverse hugs for the ignorant and fearful

— and Democracy, if there's room —

We will take it from there
to ensure a Merry Christmas & Happy New Year.

Telescope

In the middle of the night
I peer through my spyglass
at this wide mouthed whale of a world
and am monstrously untouched.
Things shall go man-o-war fashion
but dreamers like you and I may be excused
from public rooms and slime-faced figures
to draw out maps and carve adventures
curling our mental whiskers to gold ringlets,
for we sail tomorrow seafaring men
like an electric arrow shot North from the storm
in search of something precious and new.

The blessed dead-eye of my worldly scope squalls:
I've seen the beggar, the run down dog
keel-hauling, and well, that's the score.
But take your hat and faith in discovery
and deliver this message to the humbug of man:
We are going after treasure.

Things Wild

Are things wild where places he came to

with terrible roars gnashed teeth

with another kind of mischief?

Goodbye waved

stepped into a private boat

sailing in and out of weeks.

All loved someone sent off

to bed without their supper

or frightened

or roaring wild cries

or staring without eyes

into a yellow magic trick: be still.

Are things wild where nights and days tumble

into weeks

where years sail off to sea

where vines that grew and grew became walls

where the forest grew rooms over night?

How does the world smell from far across the way?

To Those Who Bunt in Kickball

Disgrace to tap such a vibrant bouncy thing
whose sole purpose is to be struck, attacked like an enemy,
launched into air. How beautiful a solid object is suspended
at its pinnacle height in the blue sky.

Where will you be when volcanoes erupt and fire rains from the
heavens and it's every kickballer for himself? I'll tell you where
I'll be: naked, screaming battle cries, kicking thousands of red rubber
balls into the volcanoes, stopping lava's flow, and saving humanity.

Timothy Carroll

2845 29th Ave S.

Minneapolis, MN 55406

860-921-1348   tmc444@hotmail.com

PROFILE
I am a passionate advocate for the poor and people with disabilities seeking an organization to match my ambitious and progressive nature. I thrive both independently and as a team member, and bring exceptional creative and critical thinking skills to any environment. I have devoted my entire working life to improving living conditions for those in need including serving in Bangladesh as a Peace Corps Volunteer and case manager in homeless shelters and non-profits throughout Minnesota and New York City.

EXPERIENCE

CADI Case Manager, Community Involvement Programs -- Minneapolis, MN   **2013 - Present**
Performed monthly LTCC and PCA assessments for individuals with disabilities under the CADI wavier.
Developed holistic and person centered community support plans to help individuals achieve their goals.
Coordinated and managed person centered services to assist individuals within the areas of obtaining housing, accessing community resources, personal and medical cares, transportation, independent living skills, and mental health services. Experienced in MNChoices Assessments and procedures.

Substitute Teacher, Kelly Educational Staffing — Arden Hills, MN   **2010 - 2013**
Provided metro area schools with effective teaching using the most current pedagogical practices. Successfully   replaced teachers on long-term leave by adopting their lesson plans while implementing my own style.
Developed a rapport with administrators and students necessary to produce a productive learning environment.

Student Teacher, Institute for Collaborative Education — New York, NY   **2008 - 2010**
Taught 11th grade American Literature and 8th grade Humanities to diverse, multi-skilled groups of students with an emphasis on college writing and differentiating instruction. Provided after school tutoring for struggling individuals. Established and taught the school's first poetry club for inspiring creative writers.

Case Manager, Jamaica Home Base — New York, NY   **2006 - 2008**
Provided intensive case management to families at imminent risk of becoming homeless. Helped this newly formed organization thrive into becoming New York City's most successful homeless prevention service provider. Successfully wrote state and federal housing grants on behalf of clients. Mediated appointments between clients and community organizations (HUD, Public Assistance, schools, courts, etc.)

EDUCATION
Brooklyn College — Brooklyn, NY
M.F.A. Creative Writing - **2010**

Eastern Connecticut State University — Willimantic, CT
B.A. Sociology, English minor - **2004**

SKILLS	**SOFTWARE**
Grant writing	Microsoft Office 2010 including CRM
Community organizing	SMART/Promethean Technology
Fundraising	Adobe Photoshop
Youth Development	Fluent on both Macintosh/ Windows platforms
Teaching	

www.ingramcontent.com/pod-product-compliance
Lightning Source LLC
Chambersburg PA
CBHW051048030426

42339CB00006B/244